Reading
Readiness
Inventory

Wayne Weimer
Anne Weimer

Albuquerque Public Schools

Charles E. Merrill Publishing Company
A Bell & Howell Company
Columbus   Toronto   London   Sydney

The Charles E. Merrill
Comprehensive Reading Program
Arthur W. Heilman, Consulting Editor

Published by
Charles E. Merrill Publishing Company
A Bell & Howell Company
Columbus, Ohio 43216

ISBN: 0-675-08547-0

Library of Congress Catalog Card Number:
76-51955

1 2 3 4 5 6 7—82 81 80 79 78 77

Printed in the United States of America

Preface

The Reading Readiness Inventory (RRI) has been designed for classroom teachers in the kindergarten and the primary grades who are concerned with an individual diagnostic approach. Designed for either individual or group administration, the RRI aids in assessing readiness for reading for each individual. As a group test, it maintains its reliability while reducing administration time to insignificance. The group test becomes a part of the planned activities during the first weeks and other selected periods of the school year.

It is suggested that teachers:

1. Read the entire manual carefully.
2. Administer the RRI as an individual test before attempting group administration.
3. Use other measures (observations, teacher-constructed tests, and parent interviews) as supplements to the RRI.

Whenever a pattern of deficiencies exists, teachers must provide activities which will aid the student in overcoming his or her difficulties. Part Three contains suggested activities with which the teacher may want to begin.

W.R.W.
A.M.W.

Contents

Introduction   ix

General Information   xiii
Specific Instructions   xiv
Sample Summary Record   xv

Part One: Reading Readiness Inventory   1

Group Inventory Record	5	
Summary Record	7	
Subtests	Form A	Form B
1. Using the Pencil	9	35
2. Visual Motor Activity	10	36
3. Auditory Discrimination	13	39
4. Verbalization	17	43
5. Categories	18	44
6. Reversals	19	45
7. Matching Words	23	49
8. Recognizing Words	27	53
9. Recognizing Words	28	54
10. Reproducing Words	31	57

Part Two: Ongoing Evaluation   59

Part Three: Suggested Readiness Activities   71

Activity Resources   109

References   110

Introduction

Readiness for learning is a complex and highly controversial topic. The dimensions of readiness are unclear, and behavioral scientists disagree as to the significance of the concept.

Since our society is entrenched in the tradition of starting all children in the first grade at the age of six years, chronological age has become the only criterion for deciding if children are "ready" for this new and exciting adventure. Of course, chronological age will be the only characteristic that many of these children have in common, even though it is the least important in assessing whether or not each child has the psychological, intellectual, and neurological maturity to profit from the school experience (Zintz,1970).

Gmeiner (1965) writes that readiness is having "lived long enough to create, to play, to make friends, to feel good about oneself, to be able to listen, to be willing to talk, and to have the ability to think." Equating the principles of readiness and maturation not only muddies the conceptual waters but also makes it difficult for the school to appreciate that insufficient readiness may reflect pupils' inadequate prior learning because of inappropriate or ineffective instructional methods. Thus, lack of maturation can become a convenient scapegoat whenever children manifest insufficient readiness to learn (Ausubel,1959).

Where lack of readiness is a product of lack of training, the teacher must increase readiness. Maturation alone will not manifest in the child the readiness to speak grammatically, read skillfully, and compose limericks with poetic skill. Maturation, as interpreted by Piaget (1952), Koffka (1928), and Hebb (1949), is contingent on functioning, which in turn is fostered by experience and training. Maturation unfolds in continuous interaction and stimulation. Thus, the educator cannot afford to wait passively for maturation to occur, nor should he/she expose the child to the kind of instruction that is clearly inappropriate at his/her stage of growth. Teaching methods should be matched to the child's specific developmental needs (deHirsch,1966).

The movement of the hands, eyes, and organs of speech is of great importance for school readiness. Gesell (1946) points out that the child's manner of handling writing and drawing tools is highly dependent upon the degree of development of the neuromuscular system.

A child's first learnings, motor learnings, provide him/her with primitive motor patterns of behavior which are largely independent of volitional or cognitive control. As these early motor learnings blend with the child's evolving visual and auditory learnings, a readiness for learning or a foundation for formal learning is developed.

Too often the influence of these early motor learnings on the child's readiness for learning is overlooked or discounted. The influence of these early learnings must be recognized. Both remedial and preventive programs of motor patterning should be an integral part of the school curriculum.

Frequently a child's preschool motor learning experiences have been inappropriate. As a result, his/her visual, auditory, and motor learning skills are not sufficiently developed so that he/she has readiness for learning. The child is inattentive, distractable, and does not relate consistently and significantly to his/her environment (McLeod, 1968).

As the child develops physically, more complex activities such as perception, symbolic manipulation, concept formation, and the like will develop (Piaget, 1952). However, these more complex activities depend upon and utilize in their acquisition the more basic motor learnings. Insofar as the early motor learning is deficient, the more complex learnings will be impeded and retarded. The motor activities of the child, therefore, become not only important for their own sake, but for the contribution which they make to the more complex activities which the child will be required to perform at later stages.

Inhelder and Piaget (1958) identify four distinct stages of intellectual development: (1) the sensorimotor period, (2) the preoperational period, (3) the period of concrete operations, and (4) the period of operational thought.

The sensorimotor period begins at birth and lasts until the child is about two years old. The child begins to receive information through his/her sense organs concerning the world around him/her. Gradually, motor responses develop. In time visual, auditory, tactual, and kinesthetic sensations become organized into coordinated patterns of action. Piaget calls these patterns of action sensorimotor schemata.

The preoperational stage extends until about the fourth year. During this phase, the child's thinking becomes increasingly like that of an adult. The learning of language provides the child with symbols and labels for processing data from varied experiences.

During the stage of concrete operations, which extends until the child is approximately eleven years old, the child's thinking, though increasingly more logical and systematic, is nevertheless limited to what he/she has experienced.

There are certain obvious mental, physical, and emotional factors that dictate how ready an individual is to learn. Learning to read depends, among other things, on the degree to which a child can maintain certain postural adjustments, has ability in binocular fusion, is able to discriminate between various shapes, can interact with people, is able to relate sounds to their appropriate symbols, and reviews the product of reading as desirable (Smith, 1969).

It would be unrealistic to expect children with divergent interests, different backgrounds, and unequal linguistic ability, physical stamina, hearing ability, vision, and intellect to grow at the same rate in such a complicated set of skills and abilities as those involved in learning to read. Bond and Tinker (1957) feel that "there are many important ingredients that are learned and, therefore, susceptible to guidance. To a large degree, reading readiness can and should be taught." Some children will need a few weeks of readiness and others may need as long as a year.

Hildreth (1950) points out that research findings support a readiness program. Studies show that more mature and better prepared children do much better academically. The concerns of the first grade teacher, then, should be evaluation of children's skills when they come to first grade, determination of their degree of readiness for the reading act, and certainty that those who give evidence of the lack of readiness in any area have the opportunity to develop needed skills before they are presented formal reading tasks. Children who are taught reading when they are ready will generally learn easily and read a great deal. Teaching reading before a child is ready may result in failure to achieve what the school perceives as set standards.

Many authorities discuss physical, intellectual, and emotional readiness. The assessment of physical-neurological factors, including vision and hearing, auditory and visual discrimination, eye-hand coordination and general physical functioning is essential. Cognitive development as well as the interrelationship of the cognitive, affective, and psychomotor abilities must also be of concern.

The Reading Readiness Inventory is an instrument designed to aid in assessing the child's overall behavioral organization. Along with informal observations it can give the teacher a picture of the perceptual-motor and oral language development of each individual in his or her class.

Once assessment is made, further testing may be indicated. Supplemental observations, parent interviews, and specific tests will aid the teacher in planning a transition program for those children who may need to participate in readiness activities.

Individual assessment provides useful information but often discourages teachers because of the time involved. The RRI used as a group test has a very high correlation with the test when administered individually.

The RRI is the result of the authors' extensive studies using the deHirsch, Jansky, and Langford Predictive Index Battery (1966). In general, teachers seemed discouraged from using individually administered tests or inventories because of the time involved.

General Information

The Reading Readiness Inventory (RRI) is a diagnostic tool to be used by classroom teachers in the kindergarten and primary grades who are concerned with an individualized approach. As an instrument for training prospective teachers about reading readiness behavior, it has a potential unequaled by other types of learning activities. For this purpose, the process becomes the product.

What is it?

Each form of the RRI is composed of ten subtests: (1) Using the pencil; (2) Visual motor activity; (3) Auditory discrimination; (4) Verbalization; (5) Categories; (6) Reversals; (7) Matching words; (8) Recognizing words; (9) Recognizing words; and (10) Reproducing words.

Is the Inventory used with groups or individuals?

The Reading Readiness Inventory has been designed as a group test as well as an individual test. Studies show that a very high correlation exists between the individually administered test and the group administered test.

How long does it take to administer?

Administered individually, the RRI takes about an hour per individual. The time involved in group administration is of no significance as it is part of the regular classroom activities during the first weeks of school and other selected periods during the school year.

What are the benefits?

The Reading Readiness Inventory provides the teacher with information about a child's perceptual, sensory, and mental development. Along with supplemental information, it provides the teacher with data to be used in planning activities which will aid the student in his or her classroom.

For purposes of training teachers, the strength of the RRI is not as a test instrument, but rather as a strategy for allowing prospective teachers to study the behavior of the learner in a learning situation.

SPECIFIC INSTRUCTIONS

Specific instructions for administering and scoring the RRI are included on each subtest instruction page. Critical scores are listed on each student's Summary Record. When the student's score is above the critical score in any area, that area is a probable high risk for that child. Teachers are advised to provide activities which will aid the student in overcoming that particular deficiency. All scores range from best to worst, zero being the best score possible.

The same administration procedures apply whether testing individually or in a group situation. Individual administration time is approximately one hour per student. Group administration time is of no significance since RRI subtests are administered as part of a planned program during selected periods of the school year.

When the Summary Record is complete, the teacher becomes aware of any deficiency pattern. A sample Summary Record is included on page XV. The child tested scored above the critical score in the area of perceptual motor response. The classroom teacher, making a note of this on the Summary Record, provided activities to aid the student in overcoming the perceptual deficiency.

Part Two, an optional group of subtests, can be used as an ongoing evaluation after the teacher has planned a program for those students selected for the readiness program. The teacher, using this individual inventory, can gain added information about the child's behavior. You may make copies of tests and models in this book; in this way, you can test a group easily, or retain copies of pages torn out and used.

The activities suggested in Part Three are just a few with which the teacher may want to begin. The list of Activity Resources provides sources for many more activities which can be used in an extended program.

Summary Record

Student's Name: *Larry Rogers* Age: **6**
Date: *September* School: *Franklin* Examiner: *RWW*

Subtest	Score Range	Critical Score	Student's Score
Using the Pencil	0–2	0	1
Visual Motor Activity	0–5	1	2
Auditory Discrimination	0–11	1	0
Verbalization	0–2	1	0
Categories	0–3	0	0
Reversals	0–8	4	2
Matching Words	0–8	1	0
Recognizing Words	0–2	0	0
Recognizing Words	0–2	0	0
Reproducing Words	0–8	3	4

Check consistent deficiencies patterns.

Perceptual Motor ____✔____ (Using the pencil, copying, reproducing words)

Sensory Motor _____ (Reversals, matching words, auditory discrimination)

Comprehension _____ (Verbalization, categories, recognizing words)

Summary of needs: *Will provide short, intensive eye-hand coordination activities — tracing, catching a playground ball, and word reproduction.*

Part One

~

Reading Readiness Inventory

Form A

Group Inventory Record
Subtest Score

Name	Using the Pencil	Visual Motor Act.	Auditory Dis.	Verbalization	Categories		Matching Words	Recognizing Words	Recognizing Words	Reproducing Words	Comments

Summary Record

Student's Name: _____ Age: _____

Date: _____ School: _____ Examiner _____

Subtest	Score Range	Critical Score	Student's Score
Using the Pencil	0–2	0	
Visual Motor Activity	0–5	1	
Auditory Discrimination	0–11	1	
Verbalization	0–2	1	
Categories	0–3	0	
Reversals	0–8	4	
Matching Words	0–8	1	
Recognizing Words	0–2	0	
Recognizing Words	0–2	0	
Reproducing Words	0–8	3	

Check consistent deficiencies patterns.

Perceptual Motor _____(Using the Pencil, copying, reproducing words)

Sensory Motor_____(Reversals, matching words, auditory discrimination)

Comprehension_____(Verbalization, categorization, recognizing words)

Summary of Needs:

Subtest 1

Using the Pencil

Group Administration

Students are observed over a selected time period while using their pencils in pencil-using activities. Each student is scored individually. The score, from 0–2, consists of the number of points given to the student. One point is assessed if the student holds the pencil so loosely that he hardly makes a mark on the paper or the marks are so light that they are unrecognizable. Two points are assessed if the student cannot manipulate the pencil or if he or she presses so hard that the paper is torn.

Subtest 2

Visual Motor Activity

Group Administration

Students are given the subtest page titled *Visual Motor Activity* and are asked to copy the six designs in the space provided. The teacher draws the first design on the chalkboard and uses it for demonstration. Upon completion, the teacher scores each student's paper individually. The score, from 0–5, consists of the number of designs in which the student fails to respond to the essentials of the design. Lines should be connected; designs should not be rotated. If any design is superimposed on another design, one penalty point is given.

Visual Motor Activity

Subtest 3

Auditory Discrimination

Group Administration

The auditory discrimination subtest should be administered to small groups within the classroom, five or six students at a time. Students are seated so that they cannot see each other or the examiner. One successful arrangement is to seat the children in a semicircle facing away from the center.

The children are asked to close their eyes and to raise a hand whenever they hear a word pair which is the same. Demonstration: The teacher pronounces these word pairs slowly and distinctly: "kind—find" and "say—say," asking if students heard the same word twice or two different words after each pronunciation. The teacher does not prompt in any way.

Using the subtest page titled *Auditory Discrimination*, the teacher pronounces each word pair slowly and distinctly. The initials of the student making an error are inserted in the space provided. Only errors made on dissimilar pairs are counted. The score, from 0–11, consists of the number of errors made on dissimilar pairs.

Upon completion of the subtest, each student's errors are counted and recorded on the Group Inventory Record and the student's Summary Record.

Auditory Discrimination

The teacher pronounces the following word pairs slowly and distinctly.

Word Pairs	a	b
1. sing—sing	_____	
2. make—make	_____	
3. cake—cape		_____
4. pen—pin		_____
5. rut—run		_____
6. shoe—chew		_____
7. phase—face		_____
8. hedge—hedge	_____	
9. car—car	_____	
10. stone—stone	_____	
11. take—take	_____	
12. bet—bit		_____
13. pole—toll		_____
14. song—song	_____	
15. big—dig		_____
16. thank—sank		_____
17. shop—chop		_____
18. but—bud		_____
19. tall—tall	_____	
20. stitch—stitch	_____	

      a   similar pairs
      b   dissimilar pairs

a	b
_____	_____
9	11

Insert initials of students making errors in column a and column b. Count only errors made on dissimilar pairs.

Subtest 4

Verbalization

Group Administration

During the first weeks of school and at other selected periods of the school year the teacher provides time and conducts the familiar project "Show and Tell." Each student brings an object which he or she is familiar with and tells the class about the object. A subjective evaluation is made of how well the student is able to express himself or herself. The score of 0 is given if the student is able to tell what the object is and give details which will leave the listener unconfused as to the details about the object. A score of 1 is given if the student seems confused about the object in any way. A score of 2 is given if the student is unable to tell what the object is or is unable to tell any details about the object.

Subtest 5

Categories

Group Administration

During the first weeks of school and at other selected periods of the school year the teacher provides time and conducts a Categories session. The teacher asks each child, not necessarily at the same session, to produce class names for three groups of words selected by the teacher. Example: the teacher asks, "Billy, what are these things: horses, dogs, and cats?" The student gives a class name for the words such as animals, pets, etc. If the student cannot produce a class name which will satisfy the teacher, an error point is given to the student. Each child is scored individually. The score, from 0–3, is the number of categories where the student cannot produce a class name for the category.

Subtest 6

Reversals

Using the chalkboard, teach the children to mark an X over an object.

Example: Mark an X over the H.

Students are given the subtest page titled *Reversals* and are asked to match two- and three-letter combinations, presented in correct and reverse order, to a model. The model is the extreme left letter combination.

Use the first row in the exercise as a demonstration row. The score, from 0–8, consists of the number of rows, from 2 through 9, in which any error is made.

Reversals

of	of	fo	fo
be	eb	be	eb
ca	ac	ac	ca
gok	kog	gok	gok
pog	pog	gop	pog
las	las	sal	sal
pif	pif	pif	fip
cot	toc	toc	cot
zon	zon	noz	zon

Subtest 7

Matching Words

Group Administration

Using the chalkboard, teach the children to draw a line from one word to another.

Example: box⟍   boy
           bet   ⟍box

Students are given the subtest page titled *Matching Words* and are asked to draw a line between words which look exactly alike. Use the first block as a demonstration block. The score, from 0–8, consists of the number of blocks, from 2 through 9, in which any error is made.

Matching Words

bat dog dog son	girl big girl run	how boy hit how
1	2	3
hand hood hard hand	feet food feet foot	bell ball fell bell
4	5	6
me we we no	pot bet bet top	take take took tale
7	8	9

Subtest 8

Recognizing Words

Group Administration

The words son, dog, toy, face, then, four, plane, five, and pet are printed on 3 by 5 cards. The words "dog" and "plane" are taught to the entire class with the use of the chalkboard. Children are taught to distinguish between the two words. The teacher, by questioning individual children, is able to ascertain that the words are recognized "just for the moment."

Each child is called to the teacher's desk; the words are presented one after the other, after asking the student to point to the words "dog" and "plane" when they are presented. The words "dog" and "plane" are always presented in the second and sixth position.

The score, from 0–2, consists of the number of words (dog and plane) which the student does not recognize.

Subtest 9

Recognizing Words

Group Administration

Using the chalkboard, teach the children to recognize the words "dog" and "plane" and to distinguish between them "for the moment."

Using the chalkboard, teach the children to underline a word.

Example: <u>seven</u>

Students are given the subtest page titled *Recognizing Words* and are asked to underline the words "dog" and "plane."

The score, from 0–2, consists of the number of words (dog and plane) which the student fails to underline.

Recognizing Words

SON

DOG

TOY

FACE

THEN

FOUR

PLANE

FIVE

PET

Subtest 10

Reproducing Words

Group Administration

Using the chalkboard, teach the children to recognize the words "dog" and "plane" and to distinguish between them "for the moment."

Students are given a blank sheet of paper and are told to write the words "dog" and "plane" on the paper. The words should not be shown during the exercise.

The score, from 0–8, consists of the number of letters in the words "dog" and "plane" which the student fails to reproduce. *Letter order is of no significance.*

Form B

Subtest 1

Using the Pencil

Group Administration

Students are observed over a selected time period while using their pencils in pencil-using activities. Each student is scored individually. The score, from 0–2, consists of the number of points given to the student. One point is assessed if the student holds the pencil so loosely that he hardly makes a mark on the paper or the marks are so light that they are unrecognizable. Two points are assessed if the student cannot manipulate the pencil or if he or she presses so hard that the paper is torn.

Subtest 2

Visual Motor Activity

Group Administration

Students are given the subtest page titled *Visual Motor Activity* and are asked to copy the six designs in the space provided. The teacher draws the first design on the chalkboard and uses it for demonstration. Upon completion, the teacher scores each student's paper individually. The score, from 0–5, consists of the number of designs in which the student fails to respond to the essentials of the design. Lines should be connected; designs should not be rotated. If any design is superimposed on another design, one penalty point is given.

Visual Motor Activity

◯◯	
\\\\\	
• • • • • •	
4	
(diamond shape figure)	
☐ (square within square)	

Subtest 3

Auditory Discrimination

Group Administration

The auditory discrimination subtest should be administered to small groups within the classroom, five or six students at a time. Students are seated so that they cannot see each other or the examiner. One successful arrangement is to seat the children in a semicircle facing away from the center.

The children are asked to close their eyes and to raise a hand whenever they hear a word pair which is the same. Demonstration: The teacher pronounces these word pairs slowly and distinctly: "kind—find" and "say—say," asking if students heard the same word twice or two different words after each pronunciation. The teacher does not prompt in any way.

Using the subtest page titled *Auditory Discrimination*, the teacher pronounces each word pair slowly and distinctly. The initials of the student making an error are inserted in the space provided. Only errors made on dissimilar pairs are counted. The score, from 0–11, consists of the number of errors made on dissimilar pairs.

Upon completion of the subtest, each student's errors are counted and recorded on the Group Inventory Record and the student's Summary Record.

Auditory Discrimination

The teacher pronounces the following word pairs slowly and distinctly.

Word Pairs	a	b
1. tall—tall	_____	
2. stitch—stitch	_____	
3. big—dig		_____
4. thank—sank		_____
5. shop—chop		_____
6. song—song	_____	
7. bet—bit		_____
8. pole—toll		_____
9. hedge—hedge	_____	
10. car—car	_____	
11. stone—stone	_____	
12. take—take	_____	
13. cake—cape		_____
14. pen—pin		_____
15. rut—run		_____
16. shoe—chew		_____
17. bud—but		_____
18. phase—face		_____
19. sing—sing	_____	
20. make—make	_____	

    a   similar pairs
    b   dissimilar pairs

a	b
9	11

Insert initials of students making errors in column a and column b. Count only errors made on dissimilar pairs.

Subtest 4

Verbalization

Group Administration

During the first weeks of school and at other selected periods of the school year the teacher provides time and conducts the familiar project "Show and Tell." Each student brings an object which he or she is familiar with and tells the class about the object. A subjective evaluation is made of how well the student is able to express himself or herself. The score of 0 is given if the student is able to tell what the object is and give details which will leave the listener unconfused as to the details about the object. A score of 1 is given if the student seems confused about the object in any way. A score of 2 is given if the student is unable to tell what the object is or is unable to tell any details about the object.

Subtest 5

Categories

Group Administration

During the first weeks of school and at other selected periods of the school year the teacher provides time and conducts a Categories session. The teacher asks each child, not necessarily at the same session, to produce class names for three groups of words selected by the teacher. Example: the teacher asks, "Billy, what are these things: horses, dogs, and cats?" The student gives a class name for the words such as animals, pets, etc. If the student cannot produce a class name which will satisfy the teacher, an error point is given to the student. Each child is scored individually. The score, from 0–3, is the number of categories where the student cannot produce a class name for the category.

Subtest 6

Reversals

Group Administration

Using the chalkboard, teach the children to mark an X over an object.

Example: Mark an X over the H.

Students are given the subtest page titled *Reversals* and are asked to match two- and three-letter combinations, presented in correct and reverse order, to a model. The model is the extreme left letter combination.

Use the first row in the exercise as a demonstration row. The score, from 0–8, consists of the number of rows, from 2 through 9, in which any error is made.

Reversals

lo	lo	ol	ol
ep	ep	pe	ep
sa	sa	as	as
gop	pog	gop	gop
fes	sef	fes	sef
las	las	sal	sal
fip	pif	pif	fip
sot	tos	tos	sot
naz	zan	zan	naz

Subtest 7

Matching Words

Group Administration

Using the chalkboard, teach the children to draw a line from one word to another.

Example: box   boy
             bet   box

Students are given the subtest page titled *Matching Words* and are asked to draw a line between words which look exactly alike. Use the first block as a demonstration block. The score, from 0–8, consists of the number of blocks, from 2 through 9, in which any error is made.

Matching Words

chew chum chum chow	want went want were	were near near now
1	2	3
body tale jail body	bat dog dog son	girl big girl run
4	5	6
bell ball ball fell	boot bet bet boat	pot bet bet top
7	8	9

Subtest 8

Recognizing Words

Group Administration

The words bet, toy, cat, pace, than, pour, plant, nine, and sun are printed on 3 by 5 cards. The words "toy" and "plant" are taught to the entire class with the use of the chalkboard. Children are taught to distinguish between the two words. The teacher, by questioning individual children, is able to ascertain that the words are recognized "just for the moment."

Each child is called to the teacher's desk; the words are presented one after the other, after asking the student to point to the words "toy" and "plant" when they are presented. The words "toy" and "plant" are always presented in the second and seventh positions.

The score, from 0–2, consists of the number of words (toy and plant) which the student does not recognize.

Subtest 9

Recognizing Words

Group Administration

Using the chalkboard, teach the children to recognize the words "toy" and "plant" and to distinguish between them "just for the moment."

Using the chalkboard, teach the children to underline a word.

Example: <u>twelve</u>

Students are given the subtest page titled *Recognizing Words* and are asked to underline the words "toy" and "plant."

The score, from 0–2, consists of the number of words (toy and plant) which the student fails to underline.

Recognizing Words

BET

TOY

CAT

PACE

THAN

POUR

PLANT

NINE

SUN

Subtest 10

Reproducing Words

Group Administration

Using the chalkboard, teach the children to recognize the words "toy" and "plant" and to distinguish between them "just for the moment."

Students are given a blank sheet of paper and are asked to write the words "toy" and "plant" on the paper. The words should not be shown during the exercise.

The score, from 0–8, consists of the number of letters in the words "toy" and "plant" which the student fails to reproduce. *Letter order is of no significance.*

Part Two

〜

On going
Evaluation

Subtest 1

Using the Pencil
(And Other Related Activities)

Observations are made during pencil-using activities and during periods of activity when students are using other tools. The teacher may want to compare progress while the student uses scissors and while he/she draws or writes with crayons. Samples of written work may be saved to compare progress during parent/teacher conferences.

Other activities which may be used for investigating fine motor skills are:

1. Watch the child while he/she puts pegs in a pegboard.
2. Observe the child while he/she ties a knot.
3. Observe while students string beads, macaroni bracelets, and buttons.
4. Observe while children trace circles on the chalkboard.
5. Provide open stencils of forms for precise tracing followed by coloring and cutting.

Subtest 2

Visual Motor Activities

Observations are made during visual motor activities. The children are asked to copy many different designs during the first months of school. Papers may be compared during the weeks when students reproduced vertical lines, circles, triangles, squares, etc.

Other activities which may be used in the assessment of visual motor skills are:

1. Observe as students draw pictures of themselves and other students in the classroom.
2. Observe as students draw pictures of objects presented, such as airplanes, cars, wagons, trees, dolls.
3. As time goes by, have children design and construct a paper mosaic of large fish or other animals.
4. Provide models and have children copy short sentences from the chalkboard.
5. In reading readiness activities, have the students copy many different geometric designs.

Subtest 3

Auditory Discrimination

As the weeks go by, students may be observed while a variety of sounds are presented. Familiar sounds can be recorded and then presented in the classroom. Children are asked to identify sounds of train whistles, screeching tires, birds, dogs barking, etc.

Other activities which may be used for the assessment of auditory discrimination are:

1. Pronounce four words in a series. The child repeats the one word which differs from the first in the phoneme being tested.
   a. toy, tall, *hall*, tack (initial consonant)
   b. pat, *cot*, pet, put (initial consonant)
2. Child repeats the one word which does not rhyme.
   a. pig, big, dig, *bag* (endings of words)
   b. leg, peg, *lap*, keg (endings of words)
3. Child repeats the word which does not begin with the blend sound.
   a. dress, drop, draw, *down* (initial blends)
   b. sled, *sack*, slip, slap (initial blends)
4. Child repeats word having short vowel sound.
   a. mate, mail, *mad,* take (vowel sounds)
   b. fame, *fan*, table, flame (vowel sounds)

Subtest 4

Verbalization

The teacher takes notes whenever children speak or tell a story. Comparison is made as time passes of the progress made. During oral report periods (telling about trips taken, visits to friends, etc.) a definite effort is made to allow students to describe events in detail.

Other activities which may be used for the assessment of verbalization are:

1. Listen to children while on the playground.
2. Allow students to answer in detail questions asked by the teacher or other students.
3. Urge students to make up games and tell the other students how to play the games.
4. Ask children to tell stories which they have heard.
5. Provide activities which allow students to tell other children in other classrooms about the activities in their own classroom.

Subtest 5

Categories

Many activities are planned during the first weeks of school which can be used for the assessment of concept formation. Children are provided with concrete items such as buttons and are asked to sort them into groups by color, by size, by number of holes, etc.

Other activities which may be used for the assessment of conceptual skills are:

1. Show students pictures of people in uniforms, asking the students what kind of work the people do.
2. Show pictures of different vehicles and ask for class names.
3. Show pictures of different activities on the playground and ask for class names.
4. Discuss the equipment in the classroom and ask for class names.

Subtest 6

Reversals

During the first weeks of school the teacher notes progress made when students write, read, or speak. During number exercises, the teacher notes when students write 4 or **A** , 3 or **Ɛ** , etc.

Other activities which can be used for the assessment of reversals are:

1. Pay particular attention to the student's responses, in writing and speaking, when the following words are presented in any way during selected periods of the school year:

was	no	rats
step	spot	nip
saw	net	lap
tap	part	star
pan	tops	pit
cop	pat	pets
pin	pal	
tub	on	
trap	tip	
rat	pot	
ten	nap	
but	tar	

Subtest 7

Matching Words

Many of the workbooks provided by the publishers of basal reader series contain word-matching activities.

Other activities which can be used for the assessment of word-matching skills are:

1. Children look for the words after the teacher has written them on the chalkboard.

2. After discussing new words, write the words on the board and then ask the students to write the words on their papers.

3. Provide lists of words which are familiar to the children and have them underline words from another list which contains some words on the list of familiar words.

4. Provide activities which require students to match other objects, such as squares, circles, triangles, etc.

Subtest 8

Recognizing Words

The teacher routinely provides activities which can be used for the assessment of word recognition skills.

Some examples of activities used for the assessment of word recognition skills are:

1. After discussing new words in a story, write the words on the chalkboard, and then ask the children to pronounce the new words as they point to each one.
2. After animal stories are read, put new words on the chalkboard. The students are asked to point to words when the words are pronounced.
3. Write students' names on the chalkboard, and students write the names as they are pronounced.

Subtest 9

Recognizing Words

Many activities are routinely presented during the school year which can be used for the assessment of word recognition skills. Some examples follow:

1. A word has been written on the chalkboard and is in a list of other words. Students are asked to point to the word as it is spoken.
2. Write the students' names on the chalkboard. Children are asked to point to the student as his or her name is spoken.

Subtest 10
Reproducing Words

Children are asked to write words which they have seen at any time previous to the exercise.

Part Three

~

Suggested Readiness Activities

Gross Motor Activities

Gross motor activities will aid in the development and awareness of large muscle activity. Large muscle development often is a prerequisite for fine motor skills. Children should have the opportunity, through the physical education program and the regular classroom program, to participate in these kinds of activities.

Walking

The student walks a specified path—a gross motor activity which also results in sensory motor integration and eye-foot coordination.

Walking

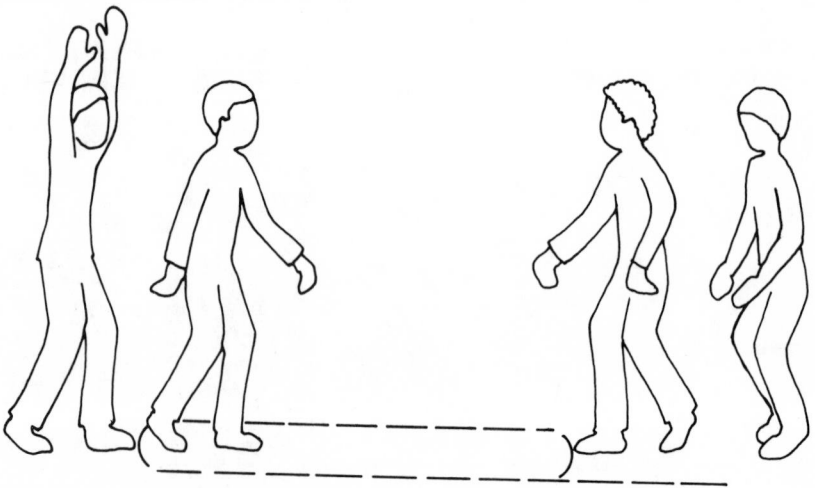

The walk relay—a gross motor activity, aids eye-hand coordination and eye-foot coordination.

The student jumps from steps—a gross motor activity. Spatial relationships are involved.

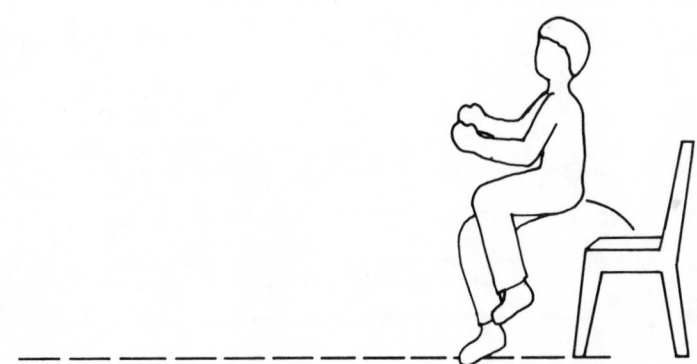

The student jumps from a chair—a gross motor activity. Spatial relationships are involved.

Jumping

The student performs a standing broad jump—a gross motor activity, fine-motor integration and eye-hand coordination involved.

Jumping

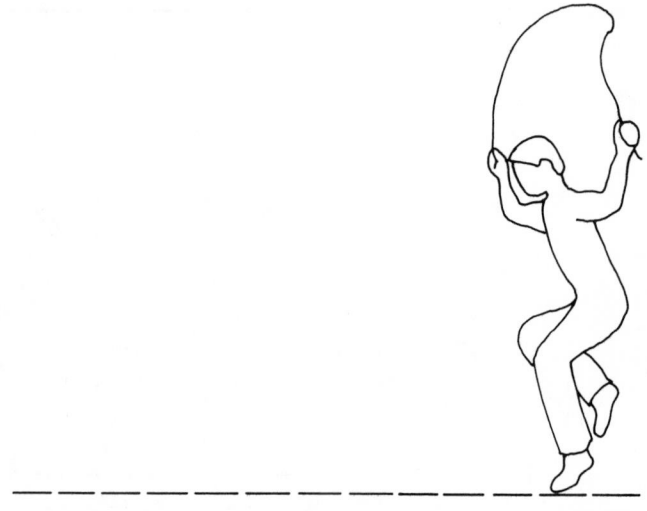

The student jumps rope—a gross motor activity involving eye-hand coordination.

Throwing

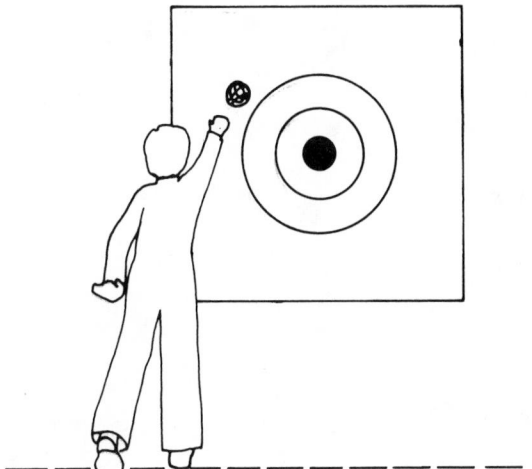

The student throws a yarn ball at a designated target—a gross motor activity involving eye-hand coordination.

Throwing—Catching

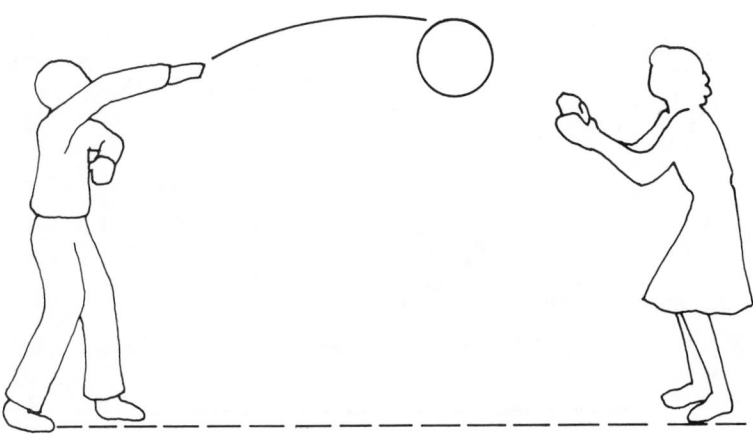

One student throws a playground ball to another student—a gross motor activity, eye-hand coordination involved.

Suggested Readiness Activities   **77**

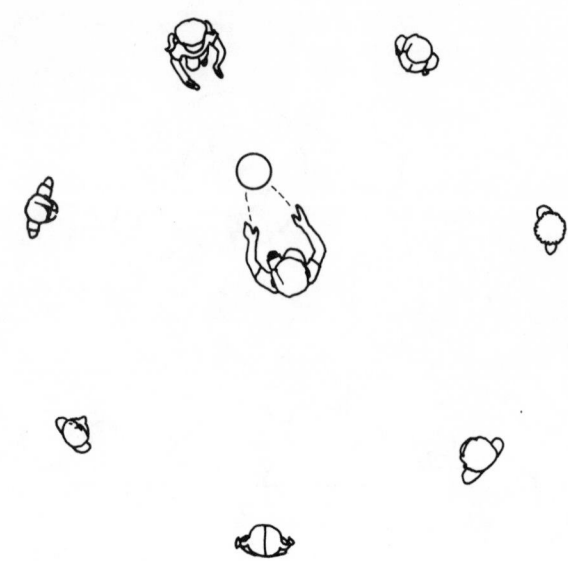

One student throws a ball to other students in turn—a gross motor activity involving eye-hand coordination.

Throwing

One student throws the ball up, the other student catches the ball—a gross motor activity involving eye-hand coordination.

Running

A student runs an unspecified path—a gross motor activity.

Running

The student runs a specified path—a gross motor activity, sensory-motor integration involved.

Skipping

The student skips an unspecified path—a gross motor activity.

Skipping

The student skips over a rope which is held in position—a gross motor activity, sensory-motor integration involved.

Psychophysical Integration

Children should be involved in activities which will aid in the integration of fine motor and gross motor abilities. The following suggested activities will help children to progress in the ability to respond efficiently to sensory-motor contact with the environment.

Balance

The student walks on a balance beam—fine motor, gross motor integration. Laterality integration also involved.

Balance

The student hops on one foot then on the other—fine motor, gross motor integration.

Balance

The student balances on a board which is balanced on a fulcrum. He/she may shift weight from left to right and from right to left—fine motor, gross motor integration.

Balance

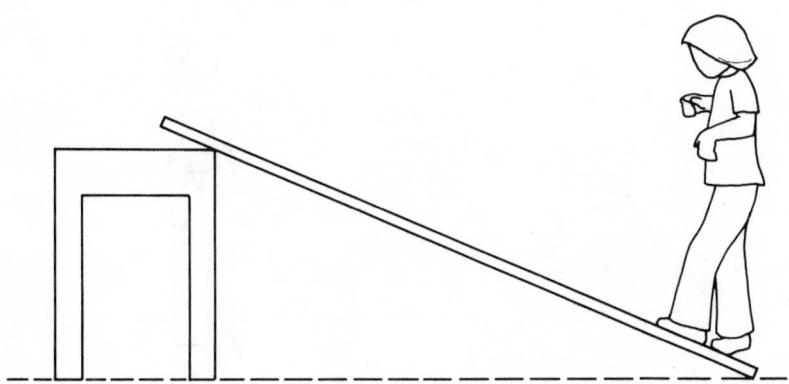

The student walks an inclined plane—fine motor, gross motor integration, laterality and directionality involved.

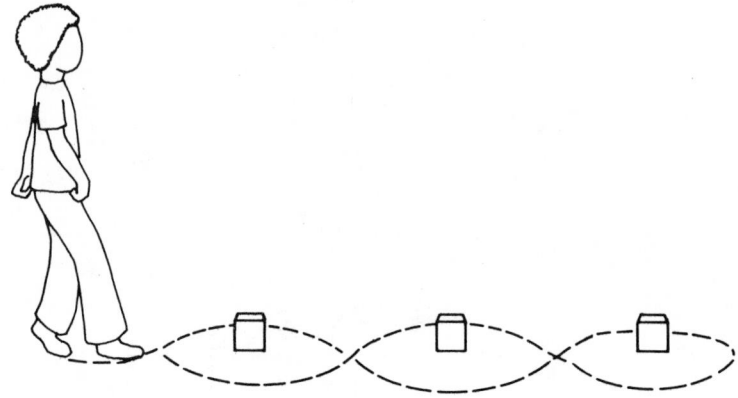

The student walks a zig-zag pattern—fine motor, gross motor integration, laterality and directionality involved.

Balance

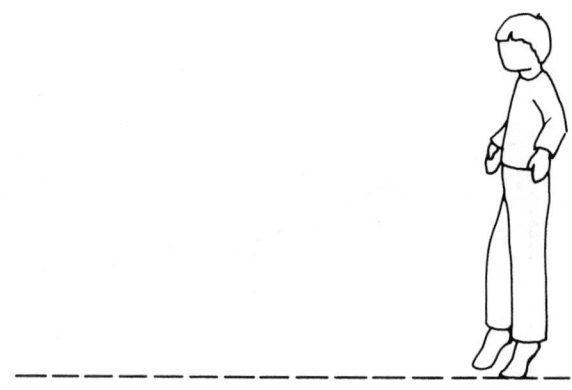

The student walks on toes or heels—fine motor, gross motor integration.

Tracing

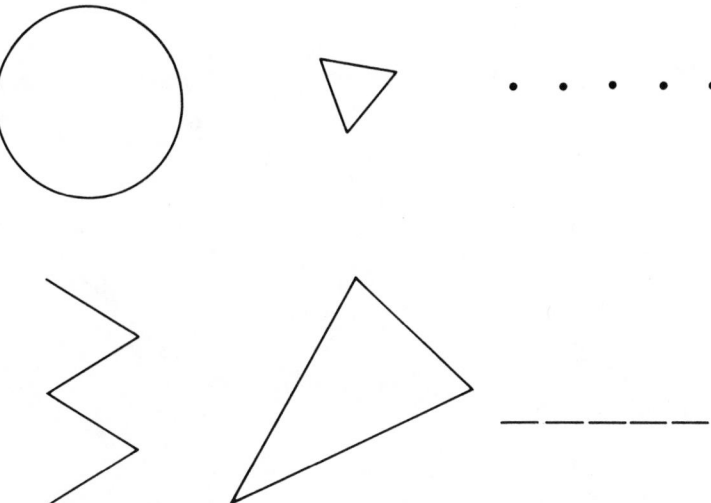

The student traces the designs—fine motor integration involved.

Tracing

The student traces the above figure—fine motor integration involved.

Suggested Readiness Activities   **85**

The student jumps rope—eye-hand, eye-foot coordination, laterality integration involved.

Dancing

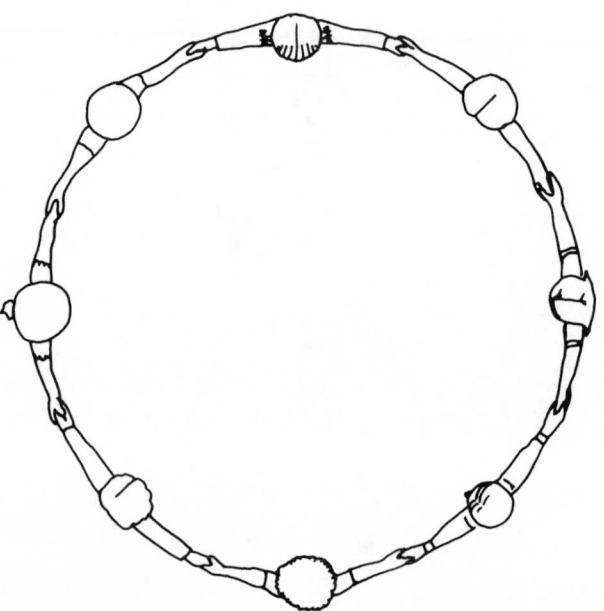

Students go in different directions whenever calls are presented—laterality, directionality involved.

Suggested Readiness Activities

hopping

The student traces a specified path—fine motor integration involved.

Tracing

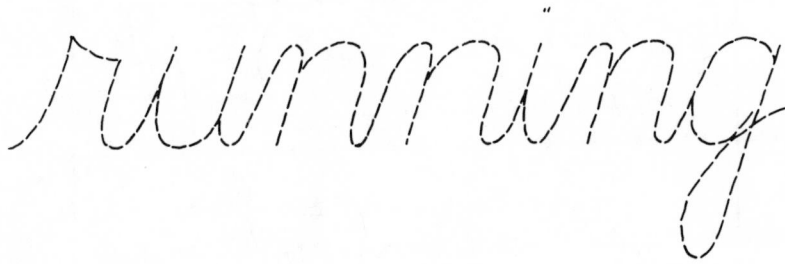

running

The student traces a specified path—fine motor integration involved.

Suggested Readiness Activities   **87**

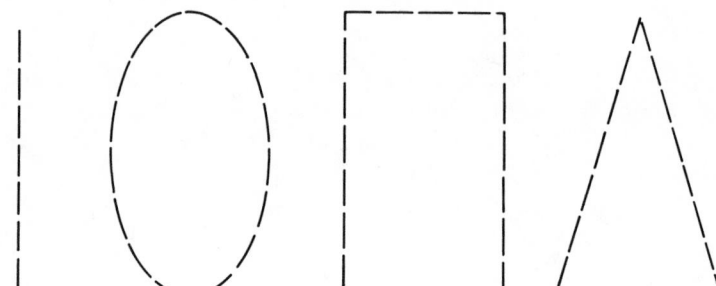

The student traces a specified path—fine motor integration involved.

Tracing

The student traces a specified path—fine motor integration involved.

Perceptual Motor Development

The child *learns* to use his/her senses. The following suggested activities will aid the student to use the auditory, visual, and tactile senses efficiently.

The student listens to rhyming words.

Auditory Discrimination

The student listens to rhymes while jumping rope.

The student learns to decode auditory stimuli.

Auditory Acuity

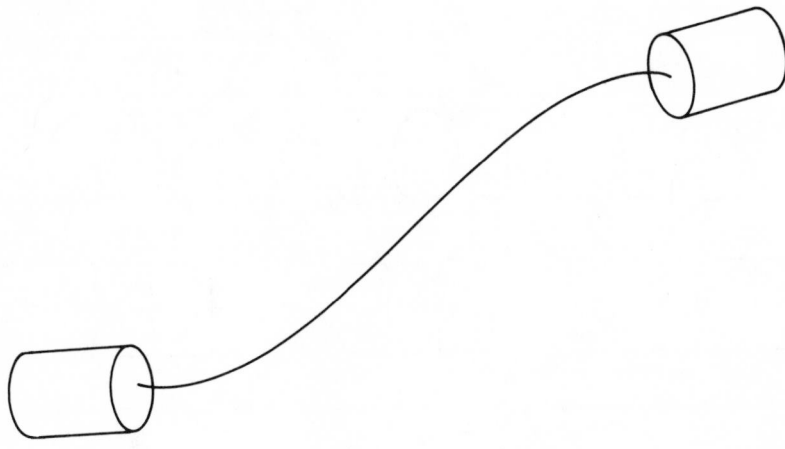

The student hears sounds.

The student tells which one is different.

The student tells which one is different.

Visual Acuity

The Snellen Chart is presented.

Visual Coordination

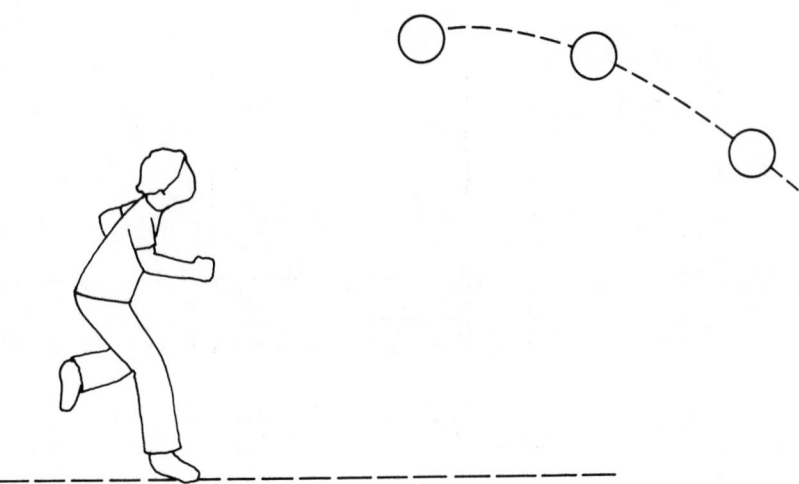

The student tracks a thrown ball.

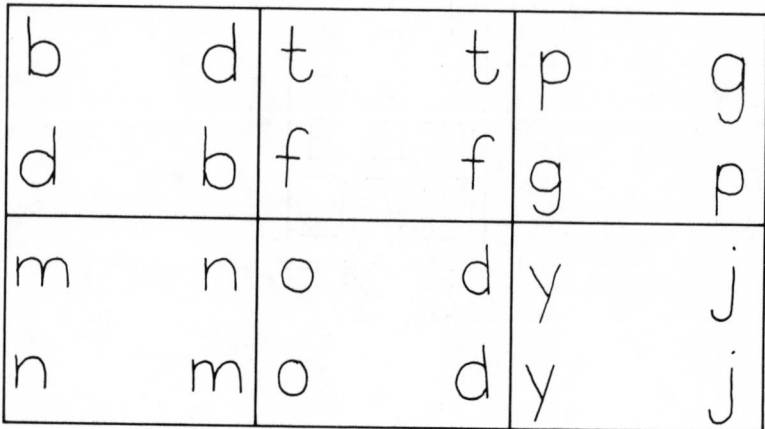

The student draws a line between the two which are the same.

---

no	no	to	to	top	tip
on	on	of	to	pit	top
at	to	dog	dot	for	far
to	at	dot	bog	fur	for

The student draws a line between the two which are the same.

The student completes the sketch.

Memory

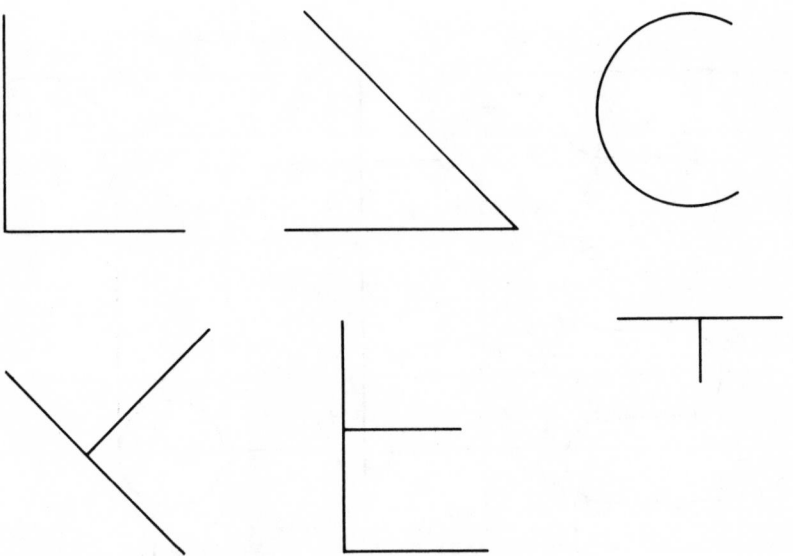

The student completes the sketch.

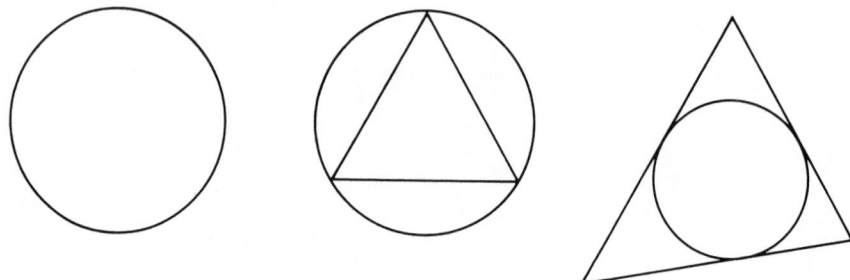

The student traces specified paths, using tools such as crayons, chalk, and pencils—fine muscle coordination involved.

Tracing

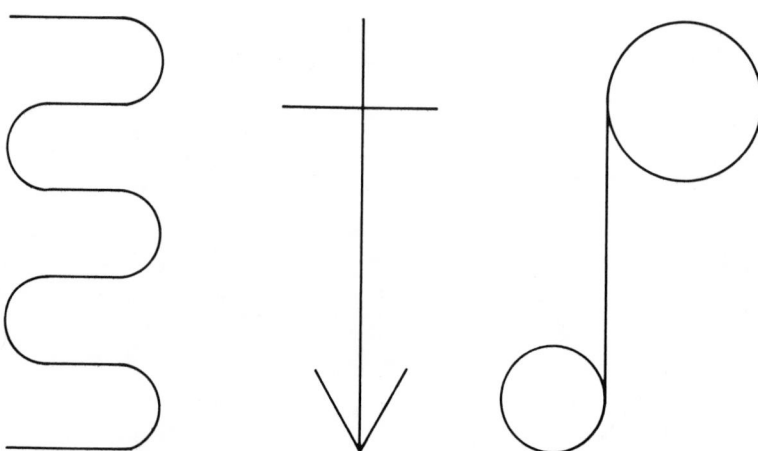

The student traces specified paths, using tools such as crayons, chalk, and pencils—eye-hand coordination involved.

1.

2.

8.

3.

5.

7.

6.

4.

The student completes tne sketch by drawing a line over a sequential path. Eye-hand coordination and visual memory involved.

Memory

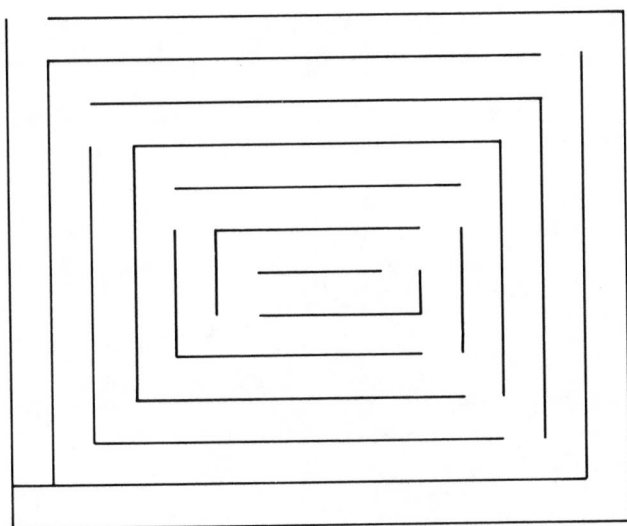

The student draws a line through a maze—visual memory involved.

Language Development

The activities suggested and the many more which are available to teachers in the area of language development will aid the student to articulate clearly, to express himself/herself, and to understand the words he/she hears and speaks.

Teacher: "What are these things?"

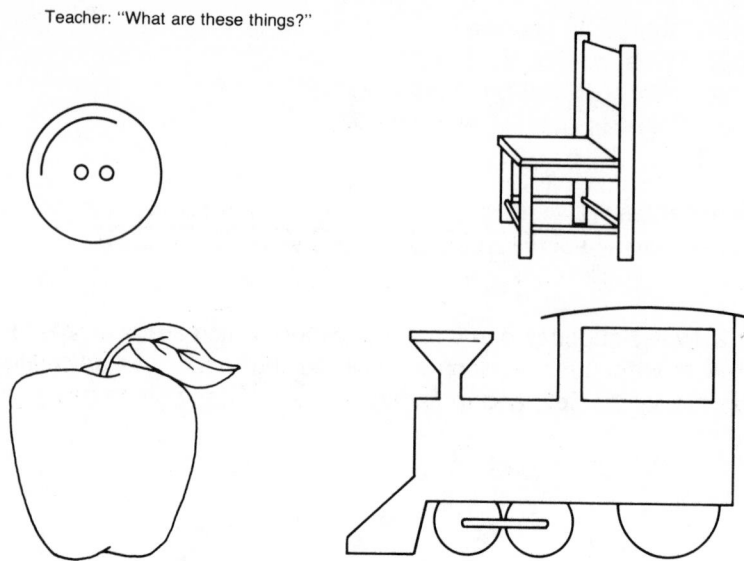

The teacher aids the student to gain proficiency in verbalization.

VERBALIZATION

Teacher: "What goes BOOM?"
Teacher: "What goes BANG?"
Teacher: "What goes CRASH?"
Teacher: "What goes SMASH?"
Etc.

The teacher aids the student in becoming proficient in verbalization.

VERBALIZATION

Teacher: "Where do you live?"
Teacher: "What do you like to do?"
Teacher: "When do you go to the store?"
Teacher: "What is your favorite game?"
Etc.

The teacher, asking guiding questions, helps the student progress in the ability to express himself/herself.

VERBALIZATION

Teacher: "Tell us about your favorite toy."

The teacher allows students to tell about familiar things.

The student points to the object whenever the teacher pronounces the name of the object.

Vocabulary

The student points to the word whenever it is pronounced.

apple   seven   cap

The student points to the word as it is pronounced.

wagon   tricycle

The student points to the word as it is pronounced.

Building Concepts

The suggested activities will aid the student in recognizing class identities. Teachers may want to provide extended activities with the objects mentioned. Example: Students can classify buttons in many different ways: (1) size groups, (2) color groups, (3) four-hole groups, (4) two-hole groups, (5) button design groups (round, octagon, etc.).

Classification

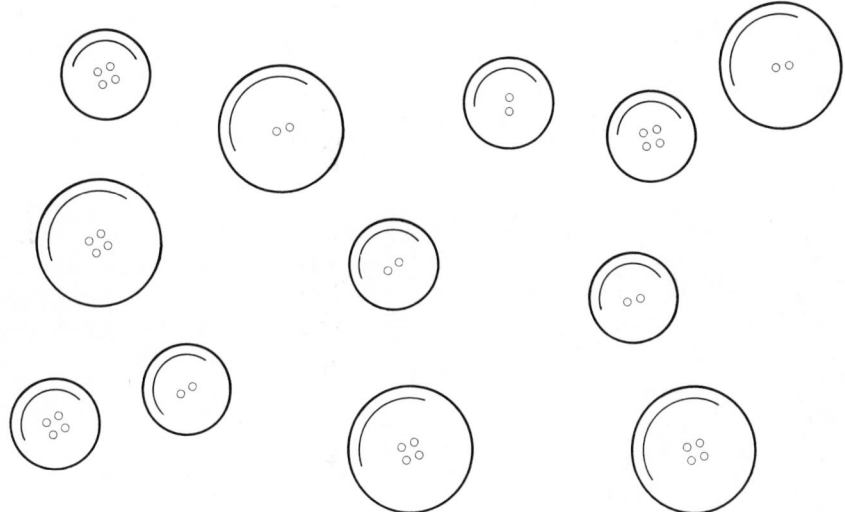

The student sorts buttons into different groups according to a specified criterion.

Classification

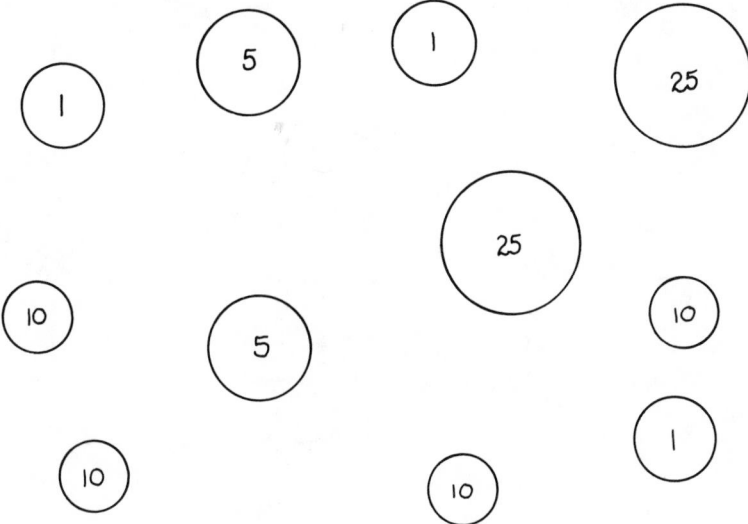

The student sorts coins into different groups according to a specified criterion.

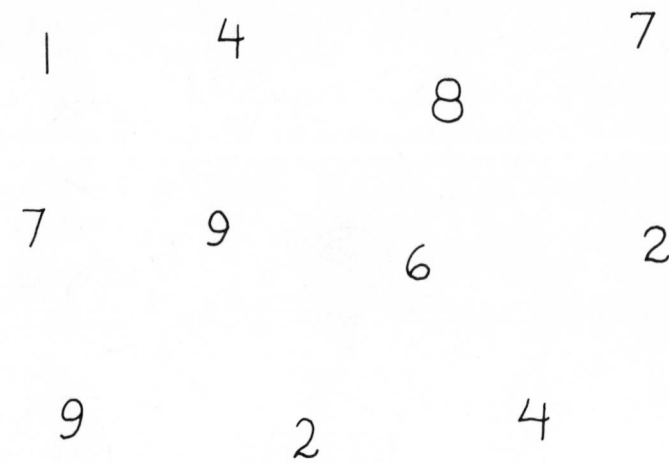

Teacher: "What are these?"
The student is asked to give class names to the objects presented.

Teacher: "What are these?"
The student is asked to give class names to the pictures of the objects presented.

The student is asked to give a class name for the pictures of the items presented.

Categories

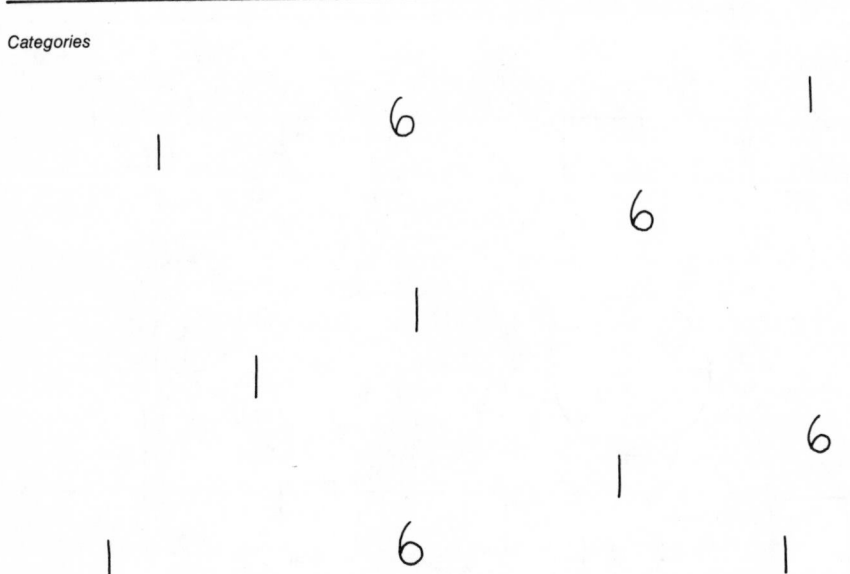

The student is asked to give a class name for the items or objects presented.

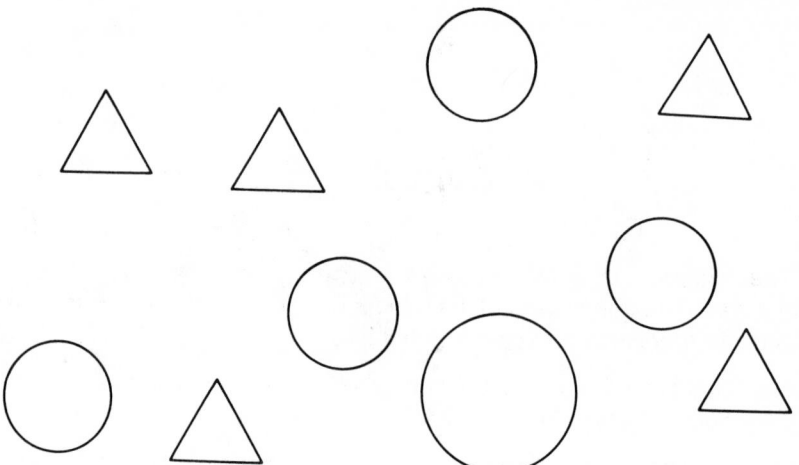

The student is asked to give a class name for the items presented.

Categories

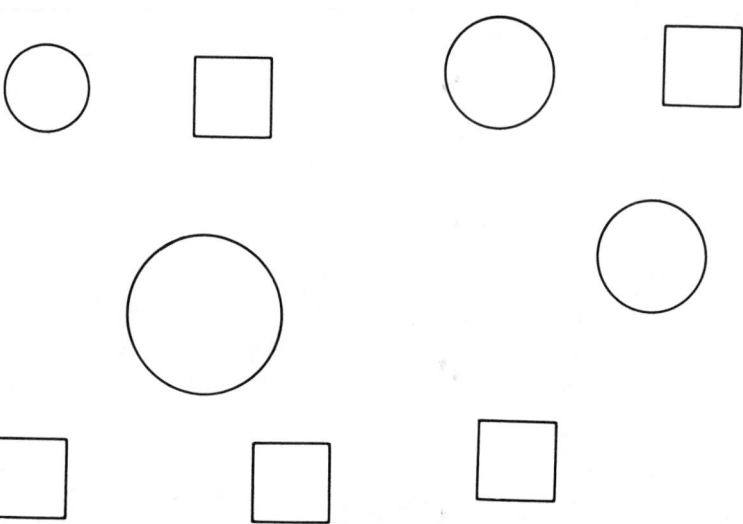

The student is asked to give a class name for the items presented.

Activity Resources

The following is a list of books which contain many activities of the kind suggested. The authors found them to be excellent resources for teachers wanting to provide readiness activities for children.

Bauer, Lois M. and Barbara A. Reed. *Dance and Play Activities in the Elementary School*. Chatwell House, 1960.

Hackett, Layne C. and Robert G. Jensen. *A Guide to Movement Exploration*. Palo Alto, Cal.: Peek Publications, 1967.

Vallet, Robert E. *The Remediation of Learning Disabilities*. Palo Alto, Cal.: Fearon Publishers, 1967.

References

Ausubel, David P. "Viewpoints from Related Disciplines: Human Growth and Development." *Teacher's College Record* 60: 245–54, 1959.

Bond, Guy L. and Miles A. Tinker. *Reading Difficulties*. New York: Appleton-Century-Crofts, 1957.

deHirsch, Katrina, Jeanette Jansky, and William Langford. *Predicting Reading Failure*. New York: Harper & Row, 1966.

Gmeiner, Charlotte. "The Kindergarten Contributes to Reading Readiness." *Reading and Inquiry*. Newark, Delaware: International Reading Association, 1965.

Hebb, Donald O. *Organization of Behavior*. New York: John Wiley, 1949.

Hildreth, Gertrude. *Readiness for School Beginners*. New York: World Book, 1950.

McLeod, Pierce H. *The Undeveloped Learner*. Springfield, Ill.: Charles C Thomas, 1968.

Piaget, Jean. *The Origins of Intelligence in Children*. New York: International Universities Press, 1952.

Smith, Robert M. *Teacher Diagnosis of Educational Difficulties*. Columbus, Ohio: Charles E. Merrill, 1969.

Zintz, Miles V. *The Reading Process*. Dubuque, Iowa: William C. Brown, 1970.